How to use this book?

This workbook is a collection of **exercises** (with **solutions**) that offer the opportunity for students to apply the theoretical concepts seen in the classroom or encountered during the reading of textbooks or any other subject matter-related material.

The book adopts **a-3-tiered-approach** to build the students' pricing competencies.

Tier 1: The concepts' broth enables you to understand the major issues, concepts and tools related to pricing.

Tier 2: Case studies train you on recalling and properly using the appropriate concepts and tools to solve a pricing problem in a real or simulated business.

Tier 3: FAQs provides insight into compound pricing issues and helps the students to get familiar with the problem solving approach much needed in the professional world.

The book offers a one-to-one correspondence with the major chapters of one of the key references in pricing textbooks: the strategy and tactics of pricing of Nagle, Hogan and Zale: 5th Edition. (*Pearson Education-International Edition*).

In this 1st edition, the workbook covers **6 chapters**, namely:

1. Price structure
2. Value and price communication
3. Pricing policies
4. Price level
5. Interactive pricing (competition)
6. Pricing strategy implementation

Part 1

The concepts' broth

Define the following concepts:

Chapter #1 : Price structure

- Quantitative approach to value estimation
- Qualitative approach to value estimation
- Multiple point pricing
- Bundle optimization

Chapter #2 : Value and price communication

- Relative cost of search
- Switching costs
- Sunk costs
- Reference price

Chapter # 3: Pricing policies

- Power buyers
- Value-driven buyers
- Price-driven buyers
- Brand-driven buyers
- Convenience-driven buyers
- Ad-hoc negotiation

Chapter #4: Price level

- Contribution margin
- Sequential skimming
- Penetration price

- Price point
- Price experimentation
- Purchase intention survey
- Structured inference
- Incremental implementation

Chapter # 5: Interactive pricing

- Retaliation
- Price-based response
- Non-price-based response
- Negative sum game
- Positive sum game
- Zero sum game
- Profitability
- Price war
- Market expansion

Chapter #6: pricing strategy implementation

- Price bands
- Price waterfalls
- Sakes kicker
- Expert resource
- Functional coordinator
- Commercial partner
- Figurehead
- Center of scale
- Center of expertise
- Dedicated support unit

Solutions

Chapter #1: Price structure

Quantitative approach to value estimation

This approach is suitable for the estimation of the **value of B2C goods**. It is based on the use of a large sample of consumers to investigate the **value** of the product or service attributes according to the different customer segments. The marketer will then analyze only the most valued attributes across segments. More advanced analyses such as hypothesis testing can be performed.

Qualitative approach to value estimation

This approach is suitable for the estimation of B2B goods. It is based on in depth interviews with relevant stakeholders like CEO, CMO, COO, to understand the business model of the customer and determine the value drivers of the product or service offered for that particular customer and ultimately be able to calculate the cost savings and additional revenues generated.

Multiple point pricing

It consists in offering the product at different prices for the different customer segments in order to maximize the total revenues. To do so, price fences should be created and communicated.

Bundle optimization

The generation of the maximum revenues from a bundle by charging different segments different package prices.

Chapter #2: Value and price communication

- Relative cost of search

This is the cost of collecting information about the product or service to be purchased. It can be high or low depending on the expertise of the customer and the type of the product.

- Switching costs

The costs incurred by customers when changing from a supplier/product to another. Example: if you change from windows to Linux.

- Sunk costs

Costs that a company can not recover such as land registration, insurance...

- Reference price

A price used as a reference by companies when setting their price. it corresponds to the best deal available on the market. This term is also used each time a company refers to another price like during sales, when the salespeople state that it used to be that much and now it is that much.

Chapter # 3: Pricing policies

- Power buyers

Power buyers are those buyers who account or a large proportion of the sales. The typical example is large retailers.

- Value-driven buyers

Value-driven buyers are those who are looking for high-value products and at the same time at the cheapest price possible. They are typically purchasing agents in companies who spend the whole day comparing and rating suppliers.

- Price-driven buyers

Those customers look for the cheapest offer regardless of whether it is the best offer or not.

- Brand-driven buyers

Those buyer cannot afford the cost of search because it is very high for them (they might not be knowledgeable buyers or sometimes the industry itself does not lend itself to trial and error like management consulting).in this case, buyers rely on the reputation of the supplier.

- Convenience-driven buyers

Those buyers are not looking for the best deal. They are just looking for a solution for a specific need regardless of how suitable/sustainable the solution is and its cost/benefit ratio.

- Ad-hoc negotiation

it is a negotiation performed at each deal/transaction. This is what happens when a company does not set clear and uniform pricing policies, it will have to discuss the terms of the offer with each customer. This occurs in B2B relationships.

Chapter #4: Price level

Contribution margin

It is the part of the price that covers fixed costs and allows making a profit. In other words contribution margin= price-variable costs

Sequential skimming

A company that adopts a skimming strategy i.e. pricing high its differentiated products aimed at high end customers can offer the same products or similar products at lower prices in order to tap into other market segments that have less purchasing power.

Penetration price

Setting prices low enough to attract the maximum number of customers. This way, despite the low price, the company becomes profitable thanks to large sales volume. This strategic option is suitable when the competition is not willing to enter a price war and when the contribution margin is either high or exceeds the variable costs

Price point

This term is used by marketers to designate a single price within a price window

Price experimentation

It is a method to test the response of the customers to a change in price. It consists in taking a sample of customers and offering them the product at a different price. The old price is applied to another group of customers which serves as a control group. Sales changes in both groups are compared. The price is changed until the price that generates maximum profitability is found. This practice is mostly suitable for online purchases where customers cannot know that they are being charged more than other customers because they are part of an experimentation process.

Purchase intention survey

It consists in asking the customers about their intention to purchase a product at a given price. The results of this survey are then adjusted on the basis of historical data to eliminate the bias in customer responses and find out the real intentions

Structured inference

It consists in designing a model that gives the profit maximizing price on the basis of historical data related to the past price changes and their impact on sales and profitability.

Incremental implementation

It consists in making a series of small price changes until the profit maximizing price is found. This approach is suitable when the other methods are not reliable and when small price changes are not costly and can be easily reversed.

Chapter # 5: Interactive pricing

Retaliation

Retaliation is the response to the attack of a competitor

Price-based response to a price cut

The reduction of a company's prices to meet or beat the discount offered by a competitor

Non-price-based response to a price cut

It consists in defending one's market share from being taken over by the competitor offering discounts by any means other than offering a discount. Example of non-price-based responses: raising the cost of discount to the competitor to make him back off or offer additional services to differentiate one's offer from that of the competitor.

Negative sum game

A game that the more you play it the more you lose and where the sum of the gains of the players is negative.

Positive sum game

A game that the more you play it the more you win and where the sum of the gains of the players is positive.

Zero sum game

It is a neutral game overall what is won by one player is lost by the other. Playing multiple rounds carries as much chances of success as those of failure.

Profitability

Revenues-costs

Price war

Recurrent price cuts by the competitors. Each time one of them cuts its prices, the competition responds with an equal or larger price cut.

Market expansion

It consists in increasing the size of the customer base. This could be achieved by several ways like product innovation and improvement of service. Price cuts may also be used for this aim but in this case the players will gain in market size at the expense of margins.

Chapter #6: pricing strategy implementation

Price bands

A statistical methods aiming at determining the proportion of price variation stemming from legitimate factors such as level of service, order size….and the proportion of price variance that is not explained which is related to pricing discrepancies. The latter part should be minimized.

Price waterfalls

It is a technique used to identify the actual price by subtracting all the price reductions offered to the customer/distributor.

Sakes kicker

A sales kicker is a profitability factor used to multiply the rewards of the sales representatives or their losses. This factor rewards value not volume and it equals 1/contribution margin.

Expert resource

An expert resource is a pricing function that consists in delivering data analysis, project management services and potentially change management services, required for a price change.

Functional coordinator

A functional coordinator is a pricing function that consists in liaising the different actors involved in the pricing decision making process, typically in case of related business units. The functional coordinator is also responsible of the monitoring of the execution of the price decisions.

Commercial partner

A commercial partner is a person who is accountable both for the design and implementation of the pricing strategy.

Figurehead

A figurehead is a person who can decide about the price but has no power to enforce this decision.

Center of scale

An organizational structure where the pricing function is managed at the corporate level and the implementation is enforced Top-down. The business units only execute the designed strategy.

Center of expertise

A center of expertise is an organizational structure where the pricing function involves both the top management and the business units. Typically, a functional coordinator links the different actors and ensures the monitoring of the implementation.

Dedicated support unit

A dedicated support unit is an organizational structure where pricing is managed at the business unit level. Each business unit has a pricing responsible, typically a commercial partner or a resource expert.

Part 2

Cases

Tasty pizza: What?, Where?, and How much?

A pizza takeaway restaurant offers the following products:

- Small pizza (80 g): 5 Dt
- Large pizza: (300 g) 14 Dt

The restaurant sells daily an average of 50 units of the small pizza and 50 units of the large pizza.

1- How can the company modify its offer to maximize its revenues?

The restaurant also offers fries and beverages as follows:

- Fries: 1 Dt
- Soda: 1 Dt
- Water: 1 DT
- Juice: 2 Dt

2- The owner wants to offer packages and he is open to change the pricing but he is unsure about several questions:
   a) Should he make the offer of packaged items the only option to the consumers or should he keep the individual items as they are and add the package possibility? Justify your answer
   b) What are the different packages he can offer, suggest 3 relevant packages
   c) At what prices should each package be sold, explain.

3- The shop owner wants also to add home-delivery service. He thinks it would increase customer satisfaction because the waiting time in the restaurant will be eliminated.

    a. What type of analyses should the company perform in order to know about the profitability of this service?

    b. What offering and price differences should/can you add for the home-delivery segment? Justify your answer.

Happy travel's smooth talking

You have a-5-day-holiday and you would like to go spend it in the desert. You walk into *"Happy travel"* travel agency to enquire about their offers and prices. A salesman named *Ahmed* welcomes you:

Ahmed: Hello Madam/Sir, can I help you?

You: Hello, I plan to go to the desert for some days, do you have any special offers there?

Ahmed: Sure, we offer everything you'll need there: comfortable accommodation, meals indoors and outdoors, sightseeing; you can go to the Oasis, see the canyon, waterfalls, we even offer the possibility of camping...look at this package:

Desert package DELUXE

Day 1: check-in and dinner at the hotel

Day 2-3: tour at the oasis and waterfalls

Day 4: dune camping and traditional dinner

Day 5: lunch at the hotel and check-out

You: How much is this package?

Ahmed: 350 TND

You: uhmmm, I'm not that much into traditional food, can I take the package without the traditional dinner?

Ahmed: sure, but you'll lose the camping as well. This makes it 310 because you'll need an extra night at the hotel and don't forget that you still have to plan something for the night.

You: uhmmm, 350 TND sounds a bit expensive…

Ahmed: I'm sure you'll change your mind when you see the hotel, look here, see how new, how clean it is, and the view on the dunes….priceless. All our customers who went there really enjoyed it! And for this week's bookings, we are offering a special discount from 100 TND /night to 60 TND. Next week, It'll be 100 again

You: Alright! I'll take the whole package!

Ahmed: I'm sure you will love it.

1- Explain the value and price communication techniques used by *Ahmed* related to:
   (a) Gain-loss framing
   (b) Reference prices
   (c) Stages of the buying process

As soon as the customer left, the boss of Ahmed said: "You did a great job with that customer! Next time you come across another tough one, use this map":

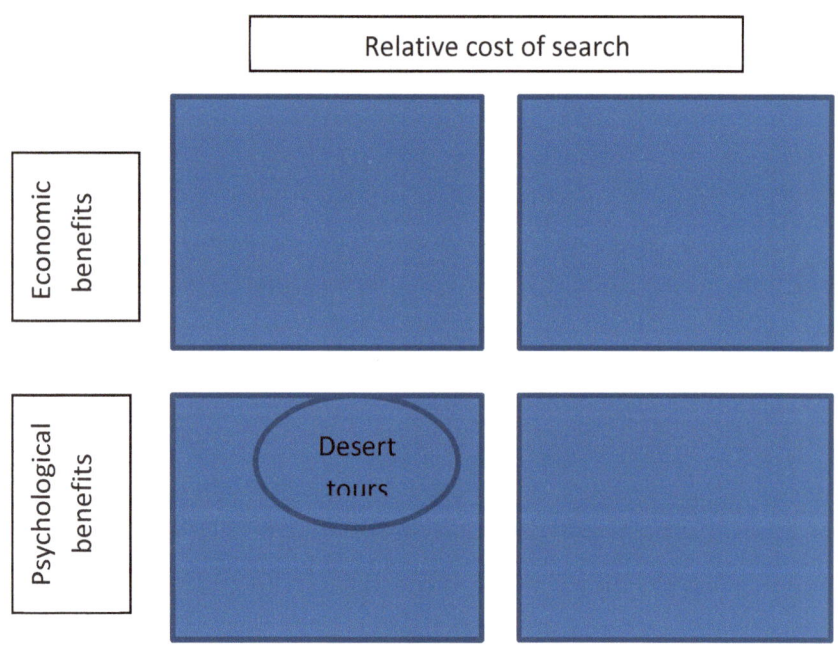

2- How can Ahmed use the map to convince the customers to buy his package?

On becoming a price maker: Selma Consulting Company defines its pricing policies

Selma is a management consultant. She owns a small company **Selma Consulting Company (SCC)** located in Tunis and she performs market research, diagnostic and strategic studies for large multinationals like McKinsey, Bain, Roland Berger (as a sub-contractor)… as well as local management consulting companies, most of them large.

So far, she has been focusing on winning deals, regardless of price in order to create enough notoriety and credibility in the perception of the contractors and clients. But today, she wants to improve the profitability of *SCC*.

For this aim, she decides to set the following pricing policies

| | Large multinationals | |
	Price range	*Policies*
Market research	40 000 - 120 000	• Depending on sample size • Payable in 45 days from the approval of the study • Currency: USD
Diagnostic studies	80 000 – 200 000	• Currency: USD • Payable in 60 days from the approval of the study
Strategic studies	200 000 – 400 000	• Payable in a-100 000 USD-installment. Payment time for each installment 60 days from

		the payment of the previous installment • Currency: USD • Exclusiveness offered if two or more strategic studies/year are ordered • On-time delivery guaranteed clause

	Large local companies	
	Price range	*Policies*
Market research	10 000 – 30 000	• Depending on sample size
Diagnostic studies	15 000 – 20 000	• Payable in 15 days from the approval of the study. Any additional delay will result in the payment of 1% of the value of the tender per day
Strategic studies	30 000 – 40 000	• Payable in 45 days from the approval of the study

	Small and medium local companies	
	Price range	*Policies*
Market research	5 000 – 8 000	• Depending on sample size
Diagnostic	10 000 – 14 000	• Payable in 30 days from the approval of the study. Any

studies		additional delay will result in the payment of 3% of the value of the tender per day
Strategic studies	20 000 – 25 000	• Payable in 60 days from the approval of the study

1- What are the types of each of the customers of *Selma* namely large consulting multinationals, large local corporations and SMEs? (*you can use the cost of search/differentiation matrix*)
2- For each group of customers, what are the intentions behind the different pricing policies? Do you think this is consistent with their types as you identified them in the previous question?
3- Do you believe the policies will be effective in generating the purchasing behavior aimed for? For those that are not effective, formulate a recommendation on how to improve them or replace them (fill in the table below)

#	Policy	Effective ness	Reason for effectiveness or ineffectiveness	Recommendation
1	USD Currency for multinationa l companies' payments	Yes/No		
2	Price of market research studies depending	Yes/No		

	on sample size			
3	Payment times and installments	Yes/No		
4	Exclusiveness offered if two or more strategic studies per year are ordered by multinational customers	Yes/No		
5	On time delivery guarantee clause	Yes/No		
6	Late payment penalty	Yes/No		

Easycamp, strong shelter and the outdoors equipment market

Easycamp and Strongshelter are two companies specialized in the manufacturing of outdoors equipment. They also target the same market segment.

The price of a tent is 50 dinars for Strongshelter and 80 dinars for Easycamp.

	Strongshelter	Easycamp
Reference price	80	50
Positive differentiation value	10	20
Negative differentiation value	-20	-10
Total economic value	70	60
Price	50	80
Net benefit for the customer	20	-20
Total Costs	20	45

1. Advise both companies on how to set their prices by indicating a suitable price window for each company

Strongshelter is a low cost player thanks to the low cost of labor of its Chinese personnel and to considerable economies of scale. On the other hand, Easycamp has built a notorious brand name over the years and is particularly popular among female customers as they highly value easy set-up light tents.

2. Given the information above, suggest a pricing strategy for each company, justify your answer

The two companies provide you with additional data related to their cost structures as follows:

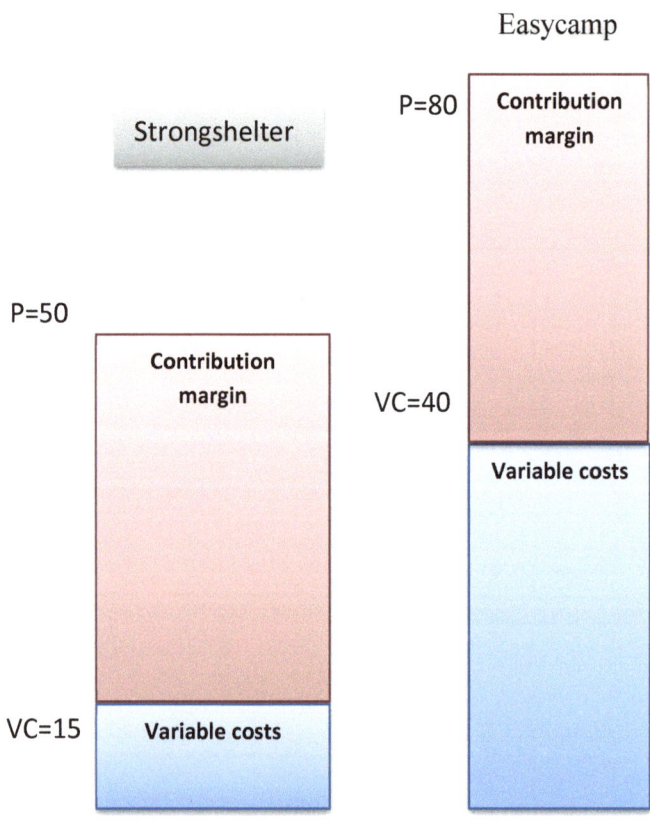

		Contribution margin (as a percentage of price)	
		Easycamp: 50%	Strongshelter: 70%
Price change	30%	-40%	-29%
	20%	-31%	-18%
	10%	-17%	-11%
	5%	-9%	-2%
	0%	0%	0%
	-5%	56%	22%
	-10%	78%	37%
	-20%	112%	49%
		Required change in sales volume	

3- What price changes (if any), should be made by the two companies: explain

4- Before the implementation of the new prices, the CEOs would like to make sure that the price change is not very risky, what methods can they use to ensure the smooth transition to the new pricing?

Since Easycamp's tents are more expensive than those of strongshelter, the CEO is concerned about the possibility of being perceived as exploiting, he asks you to:

5a- Write a message that demonstrates the fairness of the price

5b- Identify the suitable media and timing to communicate the message

Sandra & M2W: a story of price war and peace

Sandra and M2W are two apparel manufacturing and retail multinationals.

Sandra offers a wide range of products for almost all market segments including men, women, teenagers... It also enjoys an outstanding collection turnover rate.

M2W targets the high-end segment of female customers.

They have just displayed their new collections.

The price ranges are as follows:

	Sandra	M2W
Pants	89-159	119-144
Sweaters	69-129	89-199
Bags	59-89	79-189
Shoes	89-219	119-204
Dresses	99-219	121-203
Jeans	99-169	112-189
Basics	49-69	34-59

One month prior to the sales, Sandra proceeded to the following discounts

	Sandra
Pants	20%
Sweaters	10%
Bags	10%
Shoes	10%

Dresses	30%
Jeans	20%
Basics	10%

1- What are the analyses to be performed by M2W to answer the question of whether or not they have to respond to the price cut?
2- Should the response be price-based or non-price-based, explain.
3- Elaborate on the appropriate response of M2W.
4- Should M2W communicate about its response or execute it without prior information? Explain.

During the sales, both companies offered several discounts[1] as follows:

	Sandra	M2W
Pants	25%	40%
Sweaters	10%	30%
Bags	15%	20%
Shoes	15%	20%
Dresses	40%	30%
Jeans	20%	15%
Basics	10%	10%

5- Why do you think Sandra's discounts are relatively low compared to M2W's? Is this situation beneficial for M2W or not?

---

[1] The discount rate is calculated on the item's initial price.

Le Grand: bridging policies and execution

The chart below represents the pricing process of a large retailer named

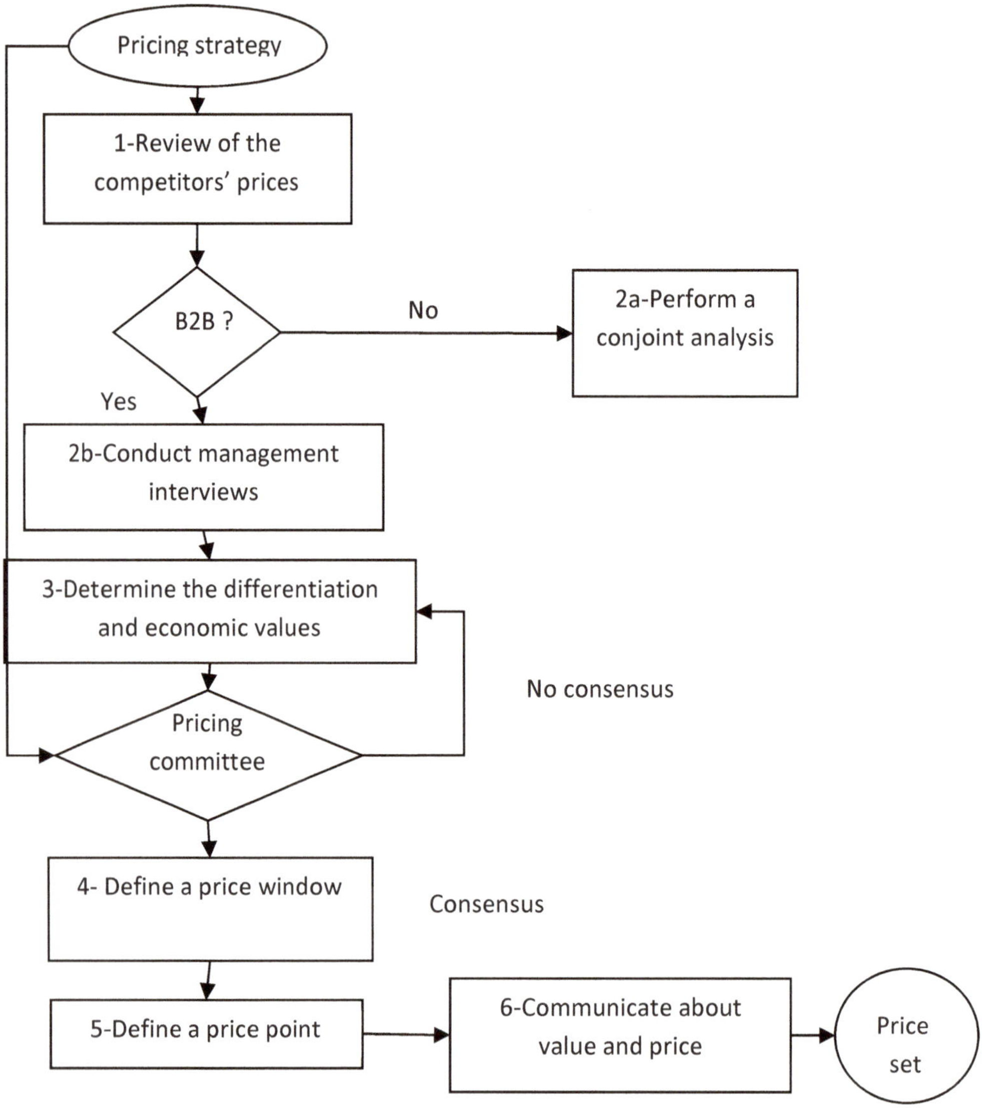

```
        ⬭ Pricing strategy ⬭
                │
                ▼
        ┌─────────────────────┐
        │  1-Review of the    │
        │  competitors' prices│
        └─────────────────────┘
                │
                ▼
              ◇ B2B ? ◇ ──── No ────▶ ┌──────────────────┐
                │                     │  2a-Perform a    │
               Yes                    │  conjoint analysis│
                │                     └──────────────────┘
                ▼
        ┌─────────────────────┐
        │  2b-Conduct management│
        │       interviews     │
        └─────────────────────┘
                │
                ▼
        ┌───────────────────────────────┐
        │  3-Determine the differentiation│ ◀─────┐
        │     and economic values        │       │
        └───────────────────────────────┘        │
                │                        No consensus
                ▼                                 │
              ◇ Pricing committee ◇ ──────────────┘
                │
                ▼
        ┌─────────────────────┐
        │  4- Define a price window│    Consensus
        └─────────────────────┘
                │
                ▼
        ┌──────────────────┐    ┌──────────────────┐    ⬭ Price ⬭
        │ 5-Define a price │ ──▶│ 6-Communicate about│ ─▶ ⬭  set  ⬭
        │      point       │    │  value and price  │
        └──────────────────┘    └──────────────────┘
```

"Le Grand". The retailer runs 4 independent strategic business units: food, electronics, household appliances and textile.

1- What is the appropriate organizational structure for the pricing function within this company? Explain.
2- What is the suitable pricing function? Explain.

The pricing committee currently consists of the CFO, CMO and COO. The CFO ensures that the price will allow a viable cash flow levels. The CMO contributes customer preference regarding buying intentions and prices as well as their price sensitivity. The COO ensures the consistency with the overall pricing strategy.

3- Are the current decision rights suitable? If not, redefine the decision rights.
4- The COO is willing to deeply investigate whether there are price leaks currently and locate them, what kind of analysis can be used for this aim?
5- Now that the COO knows what he needs to change, he will need support to ensure the enforcement of the new practices. Suggest the actions required in order to ensure a smooth transition from the old practices to the new ones.

Solutions

Tasty pizza: What?, Where?, and How much?

1- How can the company modify its offer to maximize its revenues?

The company can add a 3rd size of pizza: medium, say 120 g and price it at a price between the small and the large while ensuring that it is cheaper than 2 small pizzas. The target is the customers who find the small pizza too small but cannot afford to buy 2 of them. A good price could be 8 Dinars. Let us now assume that the same 100 customers per day will buy pizza but 10 out of the 50 small pizza byers will now go for the medium-sized one:

Revenues before medium sized pizza = 50*5+50*14= 950 Dt

Revenues after medium sized pizza = 40*5+10*8+14*50= 980 Dt

The restaurant also offers fries and beverages as follows:

- Fries: 1 Dt
- Soda: 1 Dt
- Water: 1 DT
- Juice: 2 Dt

2- The owner wants to offer packages and he is open to change the pricing but he is unsure about several questions:
   d) Should he make the offer of packaged items the only option to the consumers or should he keep the individual items as they are and add the package possibility? Justify your answer

It is also advisable to offer both possibilities to the customers as long as there is no customization entailed in customers designing their own packages. The price sensitive segment of customers will go for the package because it is always cheaper than the sum of the parts. The customers who have special needs that the package does not address properly will design their own package or just purchase the single item they need, if it is just a single item.

e) What are the different packages he can offer, suggest 3 relevant packages

f) At what prices should each package be sold, explain.

Customer segment	Package and price
Families	Large pizza+ 2 fries+ 3 beverages : 17 Dt
	2 Large pizzas+ 3 fries+5 beverages : 33 Dt
Singles	Small+ fries+ soda/water=6
	Small+fries+juice= 7.5
	Medium+ fries+ juice : 10.5
	Medium + fries+water/soda :9dt
Kids	Fries +beverage=1.5

g) The shop owner wants also to add home-delivery service. He thinks it would increase customer satisfaction because the waiting time in the restaurant will be eliminated.

1- What type of analyses should the company perform in order to know about the profitability of this service?

He should know first of all whether the customers really value this service and how much they are willing to pay for the delivery service. A market research can be performed to assess the willingness to adopt the service and being out the different customer segments and a conjoint analysis can be used to determine for each customer segment how much they are willing to pay for the delivery service. Finally, tasty pizza needs to calculate accurately the costs of the service, e.g. the hiring of a delivery guy the purchasing of a motorbike, the variable costs of fuel and so on.

2- What offering and price differences should/can you add for the home-delivery segment? Justify your answer.

The easiest way to manage the product and service components of the offer is to make their individual profitability independent from each other. In this case, those customers who order a small quantity of the product but are willing to pay relatively high for the service can do it.

The down side of this approach is the risk of losing the price sensitive segment who cannot afford both the product+ the service. In this case, a small discount can be offered on the price of the delivery provided that the customer orders a high quantity of the product (starting from xxxxDT).

The other issue related to pricing, is the costs. Tasty pizza needs to define at the outset the level of cost it can incur. This level depends on the willingness to pay of the customers. The farther the customer is, the more expensive the delivery will be. Thus, if the variable cost of delivery (i.e. hourly rate of the delivery guy+ fuel) will exceed the acceptable ceiling defined by the customer, then tasty pizza should not cover this remote area.

An example of pricing and delivery policies can be:

-No delivery beyond 20 kilometers of the tasty pizza shop

-No delivery in an area where there are very few customers (but this should not be made explicit to the customers instead the covered areas should be listed)

-Delivery service is priced at:

-Between 0 and 3 kilometers: 2 dinars

-Between 3-10: 4 dinars

-Between 10-20: 7 dinars

Chapter #2: Value and price communication

Happy travel's smooth talking

1- Explain the value and price communication techniques used by *Ahmed* related to:

(d) Gain-loss framing

Gain unbundling through the comprehensive listing of the services offered by the travel agency. This is the gain that the customer will get.

Loss bundling: the loss that the customer will get is the **price.** Ahmed mentioned it very quickly and did not elaborate on the details of this price i.e. how much each service costs.

(e) Reference prices

The mention of the old price of the 4* hotel room which was 100 and has become only 60 now. 100 is the reference price.

(f) Stages of the buying process

Origination: Ahmed demonstrated openness to hear the need of the customer. Luckily the customer was very clear about his need so Ahmed did not have to investigate it further or ask further questions to find out the real need.

Information gathering: comprehensive presentation of all the services offered to make the customer feel that this is a one stop shop and that he needn't go somewhere else to plan his holiday. **"we have all you need"**

Selection: Ahmed put forward the superiority of his offer in comparison to the other alternatives and how the customer will solve the problem of uncertainty if he books now while he still has to plan and look for last minute plans that could be even more expensive if he does not. In other words, Ahmed emphasized the cost of opportunity.

Fulfillment:

The remaining objection to price was faced by highlighting the high value offered by the hotel and the high quality of the stay there he also used some customer testimonials.

2- How can Ahmed use the map to convince the customers to buy his package
- Customer testimonials
- Backing by experts like movie stars and any other "role models" (international if possible or just local)
- Online and offline Communication material, a well-designed website is paramount to earn the trust of the customer, ideally with tour customization features.

Chapter #3: Pricing policies

On becoming a price maker: Selma Consulting Company defines its pricing policies

1- What are the types of each of the customers of *Selma* namely large consulting multinationals, large local corporations and SMEs? (*you can use the cost of search/differentiation matrix*)

Large consulting multinationals score low on cost of search because they generally work with specific partners in foreign countries which they select after a deep assessment. Regarding differentiation, they score high since they have high quality standards and specific requirements that they need to make sure the sub-contractor will respect. Therefore they belong to the category named value-driven buyer. (see map)

On the other hand, **large local businesses** score high on differentiation because generally they do have their own strategy development team, and resort to experts for very specific issues and they require them to be able to effectively problem solve. Therefore, they score very high on differentiation. The cost of search is moderate depending on the real understanding of the issue the large business is consulting for. The more they are knowledgeable, the lower is the cost. It also depends on the organization of the consulting industry in the country. In general the management consulting business relies on word of mouth and a proven track record. Therefore, the large local businesses fall under the category of value-drive buyers or brand-driven buyers (see map).

Finally, **SME**s can belong to different types depending on their motives behind the ordering of the consulting services. SMEs who need advice to face challenges will value differentiated consulting services in a similar manner to large companies. They tend to be less knowledgeable in the subject matter so they belong to the brand-driven buyers (see map). Other SMEs resort to consulting only because they have to in order to be able to claim some funding/credit...so all they need is the output in an official format. They score low on differentiation and high on cost of search. They are called convenience-driven buyers (see map)

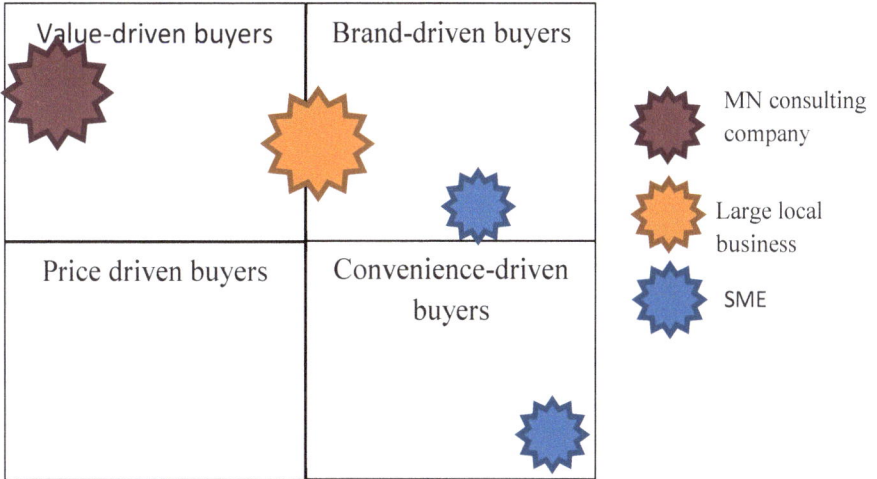

Value-driven buyers	Brand-driven buyers
Price driven buyers	Convenience-driven buyers

MN consulting company

Large local business

SME

Notice also that the service type makes the buyers more or less sensitive to differentiation or cost of search. In this case, companies tend to be more sensitive to differentiation when it comes to diagnostic or strategic studies and score higher.

2- For each group of customers, what are the intentions behind the different pricing policies? Do you think this is consistent with their types as you identified them in the previous question?

SCC has different pricing policies for each customer segment. The policies for multinational consulting company consist in pricing in USD and high while offering a high level of service and commitment: on time delivery guarantee, payment in installments is offered...Local companies enjoy ower prices but a more stringent collection policy. And finally, all customers are more encouraged to take strategic studies which is the most comprehensive service offered consisting of the market research, diagnostic study+recommendations.

These policies are consistent with the different client types because the most demanding ones are priced highest i.e. large companies and multinational contractors. Small ones who are attracted by low prices can find a reasonable price and the stringent payment policy will enable SCC to get paid by this price sensitive segment.

4- Do you believe the policies will be effective in generating the purchasing behavior aimed for? For those that are not effective, formulate a recommendation on how to improve them or replace them (fill in the table below)

#	Policy	Effectiveness	Reason for effectiveness or ineffectiveness	Recommendation
1	USD Currency for multinational companies' payments	Yes	MNCs have accounts in foreign currency. If SCC trusts the dollar over other currencies, it is their choice and there is no reason why they should be denied to get paid in this currency.	SCC can keep the right to bet on other currencies in case the USD is devaluated. A way to do this could be to remove the USD clause and whenever possible, keep the currency negotiable for each project.
2	Price of market research studies depending on sample	No	This might deter the clients from ordering the market research studies because sample size is used as a costly	SCC can offer other indicators of quality that the clients can trust and therefore demonstrate willingness to pay such as recorded phone communications or

	size		enhancer of quality while in fact it is not.	email sent to the sample investigated…
3	Payment times and installments	Moderat ely	This is a fair policy that protects the clients who will pay only once they approve the work delivered and also protects SCC who can claim their right to get paid once the delivery is approved. The only problem is that it cannot claim the payment earlier which can be challenging for the cash flow.	SCC can initiate a-two-time payment policy. 1st milestone could be at the approval of a certain percentage of the delivery and a 2nd milestone at the final delivery.
4	Exclusivenes s offered if two or more strategic studies per year are ordered by	Yes	This policy can attract and make client loyal because of the increasing competition between the	

	multinationa l customers		consulting companies. From the SCC perspective, this is very beneficial because the main target market is the contractors. They represent the so called power buyers who account for the largest share of revenues.	
5	On time delivery guarantee clause	Yes	On time delivery is highly valued by clients especially those who have a late payment clause penalty. This policy can attract clients.	
6	Late payment penalty	Yes	Same as #5	

Chapter #4: Price level

Easycamp, strongshelter and the outdoors equipment market

1. Advise both companies on how to set their prices by indicating a suitable price window for each company

Strongshelter: economic value=70 < reference value= 80, costs=20→the price window= [20;70]

Easycamp: economic value= 60, > reference value=50→ the price window = [50;60]

2. Given the information above, suggest a pricing strategy for each company, justify your answer

For strongshelter: **penetration strategy is suitable** because the contribution margin is high

Contribution margin= 50-(20-FC) = 30+FC. This is actually the strategy already adopted. But

Neutral pricing is also a very good option because the competitor's differentiation value is only slightly better than strongshelter's and most importantly, because strongshelter is currently leaving money on the table as its sells a tent worth 70 dinars at only 50 dinars.

For easycamp: **neutral pricing strategy** is most appropriate because the firm does not enjoy a low cost factor like strongshelter and at the same time its product is not sophisticated enough to justify a skimming strategy; it merely offers more ease of use to the female segment but it cannot satisfy the needs of adventurers, extreme weather condition campers, family campers that need very comfortable large tents equipped with mosquito nets, storage areas,…

3- What price changes (if any), should be made by the two companies: explain

Since the strategic option of Strongshelter is penetration, a suitable price change is a decrease. The company can start with a 5% decrease which is the least risky approach since it makes the company more profitable with only a 22% sales volume increase. If the actual volume increase is way bigger than 22%, it can take more risks and decrease the price further and adjust until the optimal price that maximizes profitability is found.

For Easycamp, price decreases are irrelevant because it cannot outperform Strongshelter who can engage a price war thanks to its low cost abilities. If Easycamp is to make a price change, it should be an increase. According to the table, with a 5% price increase, Easycamp can afford a 9% drop in sales. With 30% increase it can afford up to 40% sales drop. Again, cautious implementation is required. The company can start by a 5% increase and see how much volume it will lose, if it exceeds 9%, the company should go back to the initial price. Otherwise, it should keep adjusting the price until the profit maximizing price is found.

4- Before the implementation of the new prices, the CEOs would like to make sure that the price change is not very risky, what methods can they use to ensure the smooth transition to the new pricing?

Experimentation, purchase intention surveys, structures inference, incremental implementation and simulation

5a- Write a message that demonstrates the fairness of the price

Easycamp: our concept of tents is that it should be as strong and comfortable as a home and as light as a small bag. During the last decade, our engineers have designed one of the most user-friendly tents on the market and we still receive customer testimonials everyday on how our tents made their life easier. Today, thanks to your support, most of your contributions are being reinvested in our research and development activities to make the camping experience more enjoyable and exciting than ever……

5b- Identify the suitable media and timing to communicate the message

The target audience includes: adventurers, backpackers, young athletes, and sportsmen, i.e. young people in general including teenagers as well as people in their twenties and thirties and also families especially those with children.

 Therefore, the suitable media is:

The internet, blogs, social networks, events at universities, school clubs, gym...

For families, emails and brochures can be sent.

Regarding the timing, there is no specific timing , it should be done all year round because people travel all year long, if it is not the camping season in one country, it is the season in another country.

Chapter #5: Interactive pricing

Sandra and M2W: a story of price war and peace

1- What are the analyses to be performed by M2W to answer the question of whether or not they have to respond to the price cut?

M2W should assess the **competitive strength of Sandra**, does it have a competitive advantage in terms of design, operations...liable to make it able to cut prices further and keep being profitable?

The other variable to check is **the cost of the response** is it costly or affordable.

The following matrix guides the decision making on the basis of the evaluation of Sandra.

Sandra is strategically

	Weaker	Neutral or stronger
Too costly	Ignore	Accommodate
Cost-justified	Attack	Defend

Price reaction

M2W should also anticipate the reaction of Sandra if they retaliate. Will Sandra cut the prices again?

2- Should the response be price-based or non-price based, explain.

In order to answer this question, companies always ask 4 questions:

1- Do they have a cost advantage?
2- Do they focus on a segment served by the competitor that is so small that they will ignore the price cut?
3- Can their products subsidize each other in such a way as to generate more sales of product 2 if you decrease the price of product 1?
4- Is there a market expansion advantage for the whole industry?

In the case of M2W, questions 2 and 3 are irrelevant.

Question 1: if yes, M2W can cut the prices as long as they do not undermine their differentiation generic strategy.

Question 4:

- If you think of the two companies as part of the clothing industry, then no expansion is likely because it is already mature and hypercompetitive and everybody is a consumer of clothing not like in 'young' industries (i.e. they are at the early stage of their lifecycle and experience high growth rates) where the customers are either adopters that you need to make loyal or non-adopters that you need to conquer. *So price cutting here would undermine margins without expanding the market*.
- If you think of the two companies as part of the fashion industry, then the price cut might impact negatively the sales because brands which are associated with luxury rely, among others, on high prices to communicate their high value. So a price war is not advised.

Now, in relation to Sandra, according to the matrix, Sandra is definitely not weaker because it offers a wide product range and it has one of the fastest collection renewal processes in the industry, so it is equal or stronger than M2W.

On the other hand, price reaction can be costly because there is no guarantee that it will result in higher sales especially because of the different positioning of M2W which attempts to set itself as a more high-end segment brand than Sandra who also serves an important price-sensitive teenager segment. So it is more consistent for it to stick to its prices.

So, M2W would rather accommodate. As for the issue of the risk of another price cut by Sandra that was raised in question 1, it is irrelevant to examine this question now because price cut was not found to be the answer.

3- Elaborate on the appropriate response of M2W

Accommodation could be achieved by further bringing out its superior positioning, innovating its products, joining a fair trade initiative,...improving the quality of its products, getting the backing of some international stars such as Penelope Cruz...

4- Should M2W communicate about its response or execute it without prior information? Explain.

Communicating a competitive move will give the opportunity to the competition to respond through the same or a different action. This is the risk of communication. But sometimes, when the competitor cannot respond even if they knew about the initiative, it can be better for the whole industry to communicate. In this example, if M2W feels that it could be easily copied for example in the improvement of the product quality, they'd better keep quiet. But if they believe they could not be imitated, then communicating about their move and send the message to Sandra that they can defend themselves would have the positive impact of discouraging Sandra from further price cuts and maintaining the overall profitability of the industry.

5- Why do you think Sandra's discounts are relatively low compared to M2W's? Is this situation beneficial for M2W or not?

By its first price cuts, Sandra grabbed an important market share that it would have been more difficult to grab at the sales period. The second discount needs not be very high to maintain margins as volume has been secured one month earlier. M2W is getting the leftovers, i.e. those who did not shop from Sandra one month ago+ the price sensitive segment who could not afford Sandra's prices even when discounted. The advantage of discounting more than Sandra is the volume gain since the price sensitive segment is very large. BUT, at the same time, this is inconsistent with the brand image of high-end customer focusing company that M2W might lose due to the large discounts. The decision makers should assess this risk before deciding whether or not they need to pull back from the dramatic price cuts.

Le Grand: bridging policies and execution

1. What is the appropriate organizational structure for the pricing function within this company? Explain.

Since the business units are independent, each one can have its own pricing specialist who advises them on the pricing strategy and its enforcement. This structure is called dedicated support unit.

2. What is the suitable pricing function? Explain.

The pricing specialist could be either a **commercial partner** enjoying the right to both make and enforce the pricing decisions or could be a **functional coordinator** who is knowledgeable in pricing and therefore can advise properly the business unit he belongs to and he also has execution rights i.e the power to enforce pricing decisions but has limited power regarding the actual price decision making, which would be the responsibility of the head of the business unit. The choice to adopt one pricing function or the other depends on the general corporate policy and the management style of the business unit manager. (Some prefer to empower their employees, some others are more comfortable with taking full responsibility of the decision making process)

3. Are the current decision rights suitable? If not, redefine the decision rights.

The current three decision rights are of two types:

CFO and CMO decisions are called **input** type which consists in providing any information useful to set a price.

The COO owns the "**make**" type decision because he will decide what is the suitable price depending on the information he receives from the other two managers.

These decision rights represent the most important ones but a couple more are required which are **ratifications** i.e the right for a senior

49

manager to amend the price decision and the other one is **notify** i.e. all the operational teams involved need to know the price of the product to act accordingly when they manufacture the product, when they communicate with the customers...

4. The COO is willing to deeply investigate whether there are price leaks currently and locate them, what kind of analysis can be used for this aim?

Price leaks are identified through the in depth analysis of the pricing process. The chart could be a starting point but then, every single step and even every single customer can be a source of inefficiencies. Several analytical tools are used to identify where the company is losing money. Example of those tools: price bands, price waterfalls, customer profitability analysis, performance trend analysis...

5. Now that the COO knows what he needs to change, he will need support to ensure the enforcement of the new practices. Suggest the actions required in order to ensure a smooth transition from the old practices to the new ones.

The COO needs backing from the Top management namely the CEO and the involvement of other senior managers. The role of the CEO is to show that the new pricing strategy is a priority for him/her. Unless all the staff is sure that this is what the CEO wants, the adoption of the new pricing strategy will be shaky. Now, once everybody is aware of the importance of the new strategy to the CEO, they need to believe in it. Demonstrations are very useful for that. The new strategy is applied to a group of customers and the old strategy on a control group i.e. another group of customers. If there is a gain in performance observed in the first group, it means that the new pricing strategy works. Trainings are then organized to show what the new strategy consists in and how it is properly implemented.

Part 3

FAQs

Q1: How to estimate the monetary value of a good?

A1:

The monetary value of a good is the economic value - the psychological value. In a B2B setting, since there is no psychological value involved, the monetary value= the economic value=reference value+differentiation value.

To quantify the monetary value of a good, you need to:

1- Conduct interviews with the customers to understand the value drivers in your product/service that enable the customers to generate additional revenues or cut costs.

2- Just add the cost saving (resp.losses) and/or additional (resp. diminished) revenues generated by the adoption of your product/service and you'll find the monetary value. It can be negative or positive. If negative it means that you lag behind the competition and your offering does not provide any benefit compared to the other options the customers have. If positive, it means that your product adds value to the customers.

Q2: How to estimate the psychological value of a good?

A2:

The psychological value is found only in the B2C case. The challenge here is to transform feelings like pleasure, pride, comfort... into money.

In order to do this, companies investigate the willingness-to-pay on a sample of customers. Needless to say that the larger the sample the more accurate the estimation of willingness-to-pay is. Of equal importance to the size of the sample is its <u>representativeness</u>. A sample that fails to include a relevant customer segment will provide biased results. Finally, companies do not perceive their offer as the customers do, they may even fail to tell what makes it attractive, especially for innovative products/services. Therefore, they need to ask the different customer segments what <u>attributes they value most</u>.

All those aspects have been addressed in a standard method called **conjoint analysis.**

This method stipulates the following:

1- Segment the market

2- List all the attributes of the offer

3- Present the list to the customers to select the most important ones

4- Ask about the willingness to pay for each of the attributes mentioned as important by the customer.

5- For each segment, calculate the optimal price and volume combination that maximizes profitability.

6- Set the price as found in step 5 and adjust the offer accordingly (in order to avoid having the same offer at different prices because the high-end customer segment is willing to pay more). The adjustment of the offer can be through the selection of a different distribution channel, the adding or removal of some optional features...

Q3: What data is required to set a price?

A3:

Price setting is a two-step process:

- <u>Step 1</u>: Define a **price window**. For that you need: the reference value of the competitor, and the economic value of your offer and if the economic value < reference value, you need the costs.
- <u>Step 2</u>: Once you have your price window, you need to consider several variables to set a **price point**:
  - <u>The pricing policies</u>: make sure you are not violating any pricing policy
  - <u>The overall pricing strategy</u>: skimming, sequential skimming, neutral or penetration
  - <u>The pre-defined price fences</u>:
    - Customer segments: you can think of creating multiple price points with small change of the offer.
    - location-based: malls VS specialized shops VS rich neighborhood VS outlets VS different country...
    - Time-based: e.g. sales period, evening VS morning for restaurants and theatres...
    - Quantity-based: *volume discounts* based on total purchases during a period of time say a month e.g., *order discounts*, based on the number of orders, companies with high order processing costs reward the customers who order large quantities in a single order rather than the same volume via several orders.
  - <u>The price/volume trade-off</u>: you calculate the optimal price and volume combination that maximizes profitability. But, in practice, many costs are hidden so it is easier to use the variation data than the data itself. In this case, you need to find out how much volume you can afford to lose due to a price increase and how much additional volume you need to generate due to a price decrease. To do so, marketers rely on an incremental break even analysis for each segment.

Q4: You want to increase your price, what actions should you perform to enforce successfully the new price?

A4:

Communication with the customers about the reasons of the increase. The aim is to highlight the fairness of the increase by indicating for example that it is because of the increase of the price of the inputs, or that the money will be reinvested in activities highly valued by the customers like additional service or R&D. You can also use an index to show that if you prices are increasing, it is not because you are getting a higher margin but because the index price went up.

Regarding the date and the amount of the increase, the company needs to be clear about those two elements by specifying the exact date of the increase and the exact amount for every single product impacted by the price change. It is not uncommon that transition guarantees are offered to the customers. In the guarantee, the company commits not to offer better prices to the competitors of its customers or if they are not their clients, to align with the terms offered by the competition if they are more advantageous. In some instances, loyal customers who have several deals negotiated on the basis of the old price can have the possibility to share the losses with their supplier.

Q5: In which cases bundling is a good pricing strategy and in which other cases unbundling is preferred?

A5:

Both bundling and unbundling are strategies that enable the company to maximize its profitability.

How does bundling/unbundling enable profit maximization?

The real challenge is the difference of the purchasing power between customers: if the company wants to maximize its sales, it'll set the prices low, which will result in less than optimal revenues. If it prices high, only few customers will be able to purchase the product/service.

The solution is simple, set a price per customer segment i.e customer X will pay p and customer Y will pay p+n. But, if the product is exactly the same, the customers will not accept the price difference. Therefore the company's offer should differ from customer segment to another. The company could let the customers choose their own features as they wish but that would increase transaction costs *(not everybody is as good as DELL who can afford mass customization because they have outstanding streamlined processes and a wide network of reliable suppliers).* Bundles are designed in such a way as to gather the features that most customers value together (like food+drink, pencil+eraser, brush+painting, a doctor consultation + medicines...). This way, very few sales are lost.

Let us illustrate the additional revenues generated thanks to bundling.

	Car lovers	Mid class professionals	Parents
Segment size	200	400	1000
Willingness-to-pay	100K	25K	15K

Turnover [Single price (20 K)]	4000K	8000K	20000K
Variable cost of production (5K per car)	1000K	2000K	5000K
Contribution margin	3000K	6000K	15000K
Total contribution margin	24 000K		
Turnover [3 prices (100K, 25K, 15K)]	20000K	10000K	15000K
Bundling cost (variable cost=1K per car)	200K	400K	1000K
Contribution margin of the bundles	18800K	7600K	9000K
Total contribution margin of the bundles	35 400K		

Now let us take the same case but where the customization cost is 10 times higher.

In that case, we'll have total contribution margin of the bundles = 21 000K

Conclusion: As long as the bundling does not entail high variable costs, bundling is preferred; otherwise, the company would rather offer the features separately.

A typical example of this is when airline companies offer luggage services for free as a part of the bundles. In this case the customers will select that airlines to get the free service but as more customers select that airline, the costs of luggage handling become so high that the additional earning gained from the new price sensitive segment served can no longer cover the additional costs that their service entails.

Companies often adopt a pay per use approach to solve this problem or unbundle that feature from the package of the price-sensitive segment and keep it as a "supplement" they can purchase separately.

www.ingramcontent.com/pod-product-compliance
Lightning Source LLC
Chambersburg PA
CBHW040853180526
45159CB00001B/409